All rights reserved to Makeisha A. Williams
© 2011
ISBN: 978-1-105-16524-5

Just A Dance	9
Ultimate Satisfaction	10
The Hype	11
Epitome of A Diva	12
Div-A-Tude	13
Reality Check	15
G	16
I AM THE BEST	17
Many Snitches (Many Men)	19
My Shine	20
I AM DONE	22
Victory	23
Confusion	25
The Reign	26
Big Girl Standing	27
No Bond	29
Repentance	31
In The End	32
Spiritual Love Affair	34
The Choice	35
Can't Keep It To Myself	36
Can't Be Touched	38
The Pain Within	40
This Thing Called Love	41
Love Charges	44
Truth Hurts	45
Second Best	46

Conformation	47
Love Has No Race	48
A Soldier's Prayer	50
Redemption's Call	51
Born to Die	52
Hell's Gate	53
Death's Beat	54
Getting It In	55
A Woman's Exit	56
Flashbacks	57
Stained Glass	59
Fate	61
Sunshine's Tribute	62

For everyone who has made a mark on my life.

For Flossie-I love you and miss you!

For my Aunt Catherine Vaughn-the one who taught me to use each situation to please God, to forgive, to do what was right and pleasing to God in spite of everything else. I love you, dearly and you memory will always live on!

Acknowledgements

First and foremost, I must acknowledge my Lord and Savior, Jesus Christ for giving me the talent to write from my heart, to engulf the feelings of others and to speak to hearts. I thank Him for allowing me to use my ups and downs to strengthen others all for His glory and honor.

Secondly, I must thank those who have stood by my side through every trial and tribulation, every upset and heartbreak and who have given me insight and helped me to move on. So many people have been an asset to this project that I can name them all so if your name is not mentioned, please forgive me. Please understand that one act of kindness or inspiration did not go unnoticed.

Special shoutouts go out to my mother, Lisa Williams who was my sounding board as I wrote each piece of poetry and for staying up some of those long nights that took place to put this project together. You gave your honest opinions on what worked and what wouldn't and I appreciate that. Love you ma!

To Brotha Nature, I thank you for your friendship, artistic creativity on my book cover, inspiration and all the long, deep conversations that eventually sparked a new concept that became poetry. Although, you are NOT a poet, just "something like it" I thank you for the time we spent together working on our collaborations that turned into masterpieces. No other bond can compare to the one we formed during this project.

Tisha McMillon, my sister from the other end of the spectrum, I love you and thank you for your friendship and for believing in my every aspiration from the very moment you met me. You always pushed me to believe that the impossible could happen if I just continued to believe.

I thank two of my spiritual sisters Isis Verser and Keisha Milton, for being the women of strong faith that I held it down for me without hesitation, regrets or expecting anything back in return. Over these last few years you ladies have stuck with through everything-the good and the bad. True sisterhood is what we've experienced together because we've refused to give up on each other. Ladies, I truly thank God for you daily.

I thank Ministers Sharon Street-Johnson and Jennifer Faucette Pulliam for being the MIGHTY WOMEN of GOD that have continually set a positive example in my life and given me words of encouragement unknowingly throughout the months I used to put this book together.

I thank my spiritual brother (boo), Steven Johnson, for being the real stand up man that he is. For supporting my every dream no matter what it was. No matter how good or bad I felt, you always came to me with the word and shined light in to help me press through this journey. I appreciate you being a part of my support system. I love you, Big Man!

Last but not least, I would like to thank the following poets for their efforts and for sharpening my skills as a writer: Cassandra "Evolutions of Poetry" Covington, Wingman Gerald Green, Yolanda "Londa Lon" Vines and Angela "Angie Ang" Cofield. Each of you played an instrumental part in my life as fellow writers and as challenging me to become a better writer. May God bless each of you in the same way each of you have blessed my life.

"I really don't think life is about the I-could-have-beens. Life is only about the I-tried-to-do. I don't mind the failure but I can't imagine that I'd forgive myself if I didn't try." ~Nikki Giovanni

Just A Dance

It all started with a dance
Not just any dance
More of strip tease
That led to gripping and touching
Licking
Sucking
Juices dripping
Grinding
Moaning
Knees buckling
Grasping
Clawing, reaching intensively
For the sheets
Unable to hold on
Left with only the option
Of touching the floor
With booty stuck up in the air
Gyrating on massive hardness
As we began to release
Our bodies began to shake
Thinking that it would only happen once
Only to find I was wrong
Because he gave it to me
Once
Twice
Three times
But it was well worth it
Even if it started
As just a dance

Ultimate Satisfaction

What began as a stare at the ceiling
Became something so much more
Somehow
Someway
I was hit with memories of you
Of what used to be
And you would pleasure me
The succulent kisses
As if I was a chocolate covered strawberry
Sent in a daze that suddenly
Suddenly caused my fingers to slip between
The wetness of my thighs
Beginning to grind and moan
Thinking your hotness was inside of me
Adrenaline rushing, pouring
As I am sweating
And calling your name
I began to experience multiple orgasms
Only to snap out of my daze
Only to realize that you were missing
Missing from the action
That caused me to get the ultimate satisfaction

The Hype

Some cats be trippin'
When they attempt to use sex as a weapon
as if it's a disease curing medicine
more likely deadly as asbestos
why you think the CDC always want to test us
so let me take the time
to define
how I want to get mine
you gotta be able to stimulate my mind
cause you can't walk up on me and think you can grind
without taking the time
to find out why I shine
why I strive
to survive
in a world where I constantly hear lies
and chin checking my spies
so don't be surprised
when you can't get between these thighs
I need you to see
Its more to me
Than a curvaceous frame
that be leaving cats lame
wishing they could be free to believe
that they could achieve
what welfare recipients receive
and I ain't talking about government cheese
no need to be uptight
because you know I am right
that sex really ain't about all the hype

Epitome of A Diva

I am me-so affectionately
You are you-so devotedly
And together we are us-us creatively
Yet respectfully.
Together we have formed a force
Like none other
We are taking the world by storm
Cause we have that natural charm
Movers and shakers of this world
Letting our actions speak for us
Because word means nothing in a world so cruel
A hot commodity combined by loyalty
So strong that its inseparability
Is more than a reality
Bound together for life
By something that is bigger than the both of us
Bound by the grace and spirit of God
Together we are us-us creatively
We are the epitome of what a true DIVA should be.

Div-A-Tude

When I walk around
I walk with a nice,
Ever so sweet stride
It's so sweet
That a blind man could see
My radiant glow
As my hips
Sway from side to side
They can't help to but notice
That I'm a bonafide
Supersized
Big
Beautiful
Woman
Looking into my eyes
They become hypnotized
To the beauty that shines from within
.. ..
Undoubtedly, they recognize
That with a big woman
Comes a big heart
But not all can say
That they have been graced
Graced with the presence
Of one who carries herself
With a div-a-tude
For I am that diva
With a div-a-tude.

Reality Check

Each day I live and I pray to make it in a world so cruel
confined by the rules and regulations
of a system that is used and abused by
fiends and deadbeats
squanders and habitual offenders of a code of ethics
that is defined by those who have sworn
to protect and serve those who need them the most
especially when the pressures of the world have beaten them down
and pushed them out in the cold
while their stories go untold
yet they must face the realities of it all
cabinets will remain bare
funds will continue to be scarce
welfare will need to be pick up a lender for itself
because democrats and republicans
have a hidden agenda
seeing this society survive ain't it
and I find this all out while
eating a can of beanie weenies,
sitting on an empty crate in the parking lot of a vacant 7eleven
cause at the end of the day I am still homeless

I never fucked anybody over in my life that didn't have it coming to them. You got that? All I have in this world is my balls and my word and I don't break them for no one. -Tony Montana, Scarface

G

I am a G til the day I die
Cause I am always in for the ride or die
Don't you judge me or
Question my integrity
Cause you don't know me
You only know **of me**
Question no other about me
Cause they can only speculate
So stand down partner and
Call your dogs off me
Cause it takes a strong man to get to me
When I roll I come with an army son
So you gotta realize that game recognize game
And that at this point your game is weaker than mines
For I stand strong in all that I do
And I say what I mean and mean what I say
Cause I am a G til the day I die

I AM THE BEST

Back, back,
Back, back,
dude I said back, back,
give me fifty feet,
no, no more like one hundred fifty feet
cause you invading my space
and I would hate to bruise your face
just before dumping your body and leaving it without a trace
knowing that you just something I don't mind having to erase
in order not to catch a case
while I am walking to my own pace
refusing to be held to the standards that lack the balance
enough to put me through a challenge
because only cowards
would be willing to devour
such foolishness without malice
but I am determined to have the power
necessary to make grown men cower
as my "country swag"
puts tags on body bags
like scenes from JAG
cause only true soldiers
carry the weight of the world on their shoulders
as opposed to finding someone to conquer things for them
due to being born to survive in a game
that was built to tame
those who was distributed enough brains
to be considered insane
don't consider me belligerent
nor insolent
cause I got what it takes
to force hoodlums to have the shakes
as well as the knowledge to admit my mistakes
so when you step to me, step correct
without putting my patience to a test
because now I got you thinking I AM THE BEST
just for sending you to the priest to confess
things that you once was afraid to address
without sending your heart into cardiac arrest
while quoting scripture better than the devil himself
cause you decided to let the sins of your flesh to manifest
beyond the good embedded deep down in your soul
forcing the ways of the worlds to take a toll,

spinning out of control,
landing you in my lap
in order to set the trap
for me set you back
on a subliminal track
or take you out with a blast from my gat
due to your misinterpretation,
lack of participation,
reckless facilitation
of a life that became whack
when you committed yourself to stealing the dopewoman's crack
expecting not to get a smack
of what you thought you cause pass out during that attack
by forgetting when a chick is left on top
to make the drop,
that she also holds what can make your head go POP!

Many Snitches (Many Men)

Many Snitches
Many Snitches wish death upon me
many snitches wish they could take my life away from me
so they can take my place away from me
but if you gone kill me
at least make sure I am dead first
before you have the hurst back up at my door
because I am a soldier in an army
that was trained to train killers
and blow the brains out of gangs
that run for Saddam Hussein,
while we pull out hearts through guts,
intestines through chest,
so don't dare disrespect what you can't comprehend
cause I am well known to these streets
since I grew up in these streets,
I bang for these streets,
so I am sure to die in these streets
while cats continue to make the beast in me be released
since I am the CHIEF crucifying heathens
for pretending to be indians for no reason
 but to be beefin'
with those who be holdin' it down
on the grounds
that nobody can infiltrate my sounds
cause I am a master of street knowledge
that went to more than one college
in order to incorporate
the books and the streets
so my many snitches
could keep itching
while my crew steady digging ditches
to place them in with their hood riches
because I am far from intrigued
by swooped up weaves,
platinum rims
and fresh new gems,
letting my swag down look speak for me
making many snitches wish death upon me

My Shine

Collaboration between Makeisha A. Williams & Brotha Nature

(Makeisha)

Let me go ahead and lay this shit on line
I am living in the top of my prime
and I don't give a damn what the next bitch thinks
cause I ain't the one who needs to be paying a staff of shrinks
you better know that I can't be replaced
so make no mistakes
that will end your rookie ass up catching a case
while smoking on some base

Brotha Nature:

& stressin "like a cowboy @ a High Noon draw but forgot to load his weapon",
or a traumatized schizophrenic without their anti-depressant,
for one, they live in hater's karma, the other caught it eventually
translating: "if you fail to plan; you plan to fail" as the epiphany,
sound familiar? Yep that's you & revelation's overdue,
such pathetic-ness is obvious from one so "lowdown" I "look down" on YOU,
I'm "PRIME" as in first & foremost, one of it's kind,
subordinates envy that within me which is a purified shine,
casting rays that expose your falsified ways & like a vampire you can't handle it,
so you devote energy to convince those who lack sense to challenge it,

(Makeisha)

yet they seek me to conquer what you fail to achieve
cause I constantly give them the hope to believe
I got what it takes to extract
what is needed to execute sneak attacks
while performing acrobatics
like it's a brand new habit
perfecting my swag without regards to the standards set before me
knowing if I left it to the world, they would abort my vision; killing what I'm destine to be
which would force me to make you have labor contractions
cause I am the ultimate fatal attraction
waiting to happen
when my alter ego feels threaten
by people who know nothing about basking in the ambiance
of what was given in order to allow one to learn from life's experiences

Brotha Nature:

the best teacher that I've ever met,
hasn't "failed me" or misguided me yet,
schooled me on your type from the obvious to ambiguous,
how even the prettiest can reflect a plague this hideous,
learned not to be sympathetic to these "simp's pathetic" symptoms,
When you "have what it takes" they wanna "take what you have" with them,
its too heavy for the baggage-bundled mind, so they can't do a damn thang,
but numb it with h8er-aid, jealousy juice & Shame-Pain (champagne),
Since I'm what's "waiting to happen" they just "happened to wait" for my aura to frighten,
when they embark upon their deepest insecurity; the gift to ENLIGHTEN,

(Makeisha)

forcing their weakened hearts to tighten
at the sight of my spiritual elevation
leaving them without consolation
yet giving them the need to participate in a consecration
as if it is the source for reparations
that make up for my one-two knockout
cause I'm bigger than Kanye's "College Dropout"
in order to show I ain't the "Kid" who got "Play'd" out

Brotha Nature:

instead I "played in" this grownfolks play pen,
caring for children AND adults, days out & days in,
kept strengthening stability when I sensed the stress trying to cave in,
from frivolous fam, falsified folk,"frienemies" a.k.a. "foes in the form of friends"
the never-ending work shift that was only compensated in spiritual,
but even my savior suffered the epitome of hate after consistent deliverance and miracles,
so why should I be surprised @ your demise?
your idiocy is repelled by my modesty,
funny how we can "come out the same parts" but the "same hearts aint the outcome",
if "you've done all the above" & still aint there, then go "ABOVE ALL YOU'VE DONE",
that's why its so easy to "feel me" when its expressed from the heart,
& easy to understand why half of yall still "left in the dark"
walking blind due to defects of a disillusioned, disabled mind,
my glow only gets brighter from this point, so you might wanna get used to my SHINE...

& RESPECT it, PEASANT!!

I AM DONE

I let my heart trust you
when my gut told me not to
cause you talked a good game
which your actions would later put your words to shame
but I chose to remain the same
thinking that ultimately I could stake my claim
on something that wasn't meant to be
because you couldn't truly love me
even though I was equipped
to have you whipped,
I was your constant in mind and soul
while my body was locked in a different role
which was something I could not control
so when that day came
for you to quit acting so lame,
allowing me to read the expression on your face
I knew everything I did was a waste
but you continued to beg me to take up space
in an uncomfortable place
while some other chick continued to ride your face
forcing my heart to bred hate
that cannot and will not be erased
leaving me to be damaged goods
as if I was a murked deer thrown off in some back woods
because you could not run a risk
of the public getting a sniff of this
but in the end my story got told
all because God had control
so when I say
I don't play,
take me for my word,
cause using me was for the birds
so now that I am DONE,
you and that nasty beast can have fun

Victory

The laws of the streets
will mess around and get your ass beat
forcing you to call Kuwait for some relief
cause I am not the average chief,
I fight every battle
as brutal as a farmer slaughters' cattle
making the lungs of thugs do a death rattle,
being that I am a force that is more than combustible
without regards to immediate circumstances
of the next man cause I gave more than enough chances
to build up financial security
as long as they continued to have longevity
because I believe in utilizing equity
when it comes to fortune and fame
for all that have the sense to use their brain
because I am just another woman who had a dream
just like the late, great Dr. King
who fought alongside others for my civil rights
in order for me to have a chance to be prominent in this life
without having to deal with malice and strife,
giving me a brand new sense of hope
knowing victory can be won if one continues to stand strong,
so I must be able to disregard any hatred
that has built up in my heart
in order to accomplish what God had for me from the start
because as long as I live with love in my heart,
the ability to forget and forgive,
without the fear of failure
which gives me the ability
to declare the victory is already mines
when I was given the chance to decline
the temptations of the world
yet given the opportunity to make amends
for my many sins
so when it's all said and done,
my legacy would be brighter than the sun
because I made it my own duty to take a stance
when others refused to take the chance
to fight against the hypocrisy of a nation
that has become a contradiction of its' own foundation
in order to live within the perimeter of double standards
as if they it is fine to take up the way of cowards
instead of gracefully bowing out
so that the heroes and heroines could conquer the fabrications
that bleed through the souls of the weak

leaving them incapable to achieve their basic needs
while forcing others to take heed
to the lessons their parents failed to teach
because their priorities were too far to reach,
just because they couldn't take the heat
finding it easier to give in to defeat
which gives me more than enough reason to be a chief to a different beat

Confusion

Sitting here thinking
And contemplating
On how things came to be
What brought on such misery
Over consumed by a sea of issues
Caused by confusion

Confusion that caused me to be
Unable to decipher reality from fiction
Engulfed by the struggles of my world
Feeling oppressed by situations
Situations that were placed upon me
By no fault of my own

How could this be
Where did this come from
Is there a way to go back
Back to the place where I had peace
To the place where my heart was free
Or where I had some sanity

Release me from this state of confusion
Unleash me from this misery
Give me back my happiness
I refuse to be bound
For I will have sanity

The Reign

I been bugging
every since I was youngin'
trying to hold a spot in the game
for just a little bit of fame
while putting my frienemies to shame
because I choose to refrain
from letting their hatred give me any pain
knowing it took the love of God for me to change
into the young lady who was destine to make a claim
on a territory that I was meant to conquer during my reign
living life with my swag turned down
so that I can continue being a mover and a shaker without having to drown
at least once to stay around
especially when forced to reveal those who were shackled to falsehoods
passed down to them by their forefathers who were often misunderstood,
oppressed by their very own nature
for never questioning those in authority who continued to torture
the core of their very stature
without preparing them for the rapture
that we all know will be a factor
in the return of the King of Kings
to pass judgment on us earthly beings
forcing me to be carry my cross
in order to capture my crown
cause I ain't down with going to hell
all for some shallow thrills
and poppin' some pills
that had nothing to do with God's will
leaving me expressing my concerns for the souls of my lost loved ones
praying that on the day of Jesus return
that we'll be singing and humming spirituals
from before the negroes were free to read and write
without getting beat and tied to a tree
cause I just can't see
anyone wanting to let their soul burn in misery

Big Girl Standing

The world sees my outer shell
and assume I am living in my own personal hell
but what they don't know is, I refuse to fail
because I have my own story to tell,
their glasses are tinted
which makes their sight limited
to a huge frame
that would make most live in shame
but my swag forces all to call out my name
causing my haters and naysayers
to send in perpetrators
to fire ammunition
to kill my ambitions
in order to take my recognition
for being a HEAVY WEIGHT
that refuses to let death be my fate
while forcing those who continually put me down
to sing to a brand new sound
cause BIG is just as BEAUTIFUL as the Barbie type brand
so I will take a STAND
to knock down the stereotypes
given by the prototypes
who choose to believe in the misconceptions
that portray Lil Debbie as my bestfriend,
laziness fills my glands,
and depression forms because I can't attract a man
when the truth of the matter
is sweeter than cake batter
cause I may be huger than most,
but my ass can WALK while others roll in,
my beauty has chicks clutching their men
cause I force their minds to sin,
and to say the least,
Lil Debbie is an ugly beast,
that's why I refuse to eat her treats
so before society decides my needs
or what I should achieve
reach beyond my exterior
to find out what I see in the mirror,
while taking the time to understand
being this big wasn't my plan
but things happen for a reason
so embrace me for who I am
because I can't be cropped and cut
to fit a ready built mold

that has become old
due to it being oversold
to those who were too weak
to open up their mouths and speak
so hear me when I say
that each day I pray
that God wipes my tears away
cause for me to allow man to see me cry
as if I was about to die
forces me to question
why society is taking a toll on my emotions
when I am have always been comfortable in my own skin,
confident in my stride
and a SUPER SIZED SEXY BIG BEAUTIFUL WOMAN with PRIDE
that is always down for a good ride
to EMPOWER, EMBRACE and ENCOURAGE
true beauty even when all aren't on the same page

No Bond

Word is no longer bond
For each word is violated
Violated
So easily by contradicting actions
Causing anger to enter as love disappears
Becoming an irreversible circumstance
Yet while
Reversing a solid into shambles
How do you handle such a scandal?
When word is no longer a bond
That elevates its people to the next level of mastery
Downgrading our power to achieve what is rightfully ours
Only to suppress ourselves to the underworld
That was conceived by haters, naysayers and underachievers
In order to bring down those who went over and above to be on top
Because their word was their bond
When we begin to exercise the lack of integrity
There is no more taking words at face value
Because your actions do not echo the principles of your words
Instead our words shackle us to immorality,
Leaving the power of redemption weakened by deceit.
Now we are left to retrieve our character through our actions
since we slowly allowed our words
No longer to be our bond.

No one can ride your back unless you bend. -Unknown

Repentance

I find myself in a place
A mindstate off in a distance
A place where I would rather not be
Longing
Searching
Praying
Wishing that I had the strength
The upmost power to comfort
To simplify

Wanting the power
To destroy every pain
Hurt
Ill-feeling gained
But it is up to the Most High
To rectify
Every pain
Every hurt

Needing badly
To unleash this possessive rage
For it is as if some force
A magnetic force perhaps
That keeps trying to insist
That I must go on without a palatable solution
However I must insist that
There will be no compromise
When it comes to my liberation

In The End

Being with you was like
dying a slow miserable death
because a part of me was
Waiting
Watching
longing
to break free.
All I ever wanted
Was to be loved
But you couldn't
Give that to me
I actually dared to care,
To share my passion
My desires
My dreams
To watch you stare into
My eyes,
My soul,
My pores
With no expression
Whatsoever-a soul
So cold that could freeze
The mind just to think.
I often wonder where I went wrong,
but everything points back
to the very day I chose my salvation,
Deliverance,
My Savior over YOU.
It was the day
I recognized my destiny.
I tried taking you with me
But even then I learned
That you can't share your vision
With everybody,
Everybody ain't going where you are
So ain't any need to try and take them
But that don't stop me from loving you
As I shed these here tears,
Its not because of the pain you caused

Its to relief my soul
To break free
To give me peace
Joy
Freedom
From being your prisoner
From misery
Most of all
From not knowing what love really is
Walking away from you
Is the best thing I ever done
Because it freed me
So that I could walk
Walk gracefully into the arms
Of the RISEN SAVIOUR.
In the end
I have the Victory.

Spiritual Love Affair

All I want to do is love you
From the depths of soul
The pit of heart
Deep down from the
base of my stomach
each moment spent with you
I am mesmerized
By your charismatic ways
Your warmth
Your love
Combined with
The joy
Excitement
Thrill
And compassion
That you exhibit
Each and every moment
That we share
It is because of you
I am a better person
A better sister
Daughter
Friend
You taught me how to love
Love unconditionally
How to look beyond the surface
How to reach souls
How to motivate those around me
You molded me into a woman
Full of life
Love
Hope
And joy
I am forever grateful to you
Lord
At times it as if
We are having a love affair
But I don't care who knows about us.
I will never be ashamed of the love we share.

The Choice

To many I am a tease
A mission impossible
Unreachable from the grasp of the average man
Because I choose to remained untouched
Damaged or soiled by the poisons of those
Who refuse to seek, acknowledge or edify
The Most High,
Who is the keeper and deliverer of all those who chose salvation
Without being scared to face rejection
Understanding that being redeemed is far more than a status symbol
But a change in lifestyle
Knowing the journey is not easy
But well worth it's battles, toils and snares
Being more than a conqueror
A force that's unstoppable
Being misunderstood
Mocked
Almost crucified
Due to the inability to condone
Those who carelessly go against
The principles laid before us
Set to restore us
While accepting our God given authority
To walk in Holy Boldness as His chosen
So call me what you please
Cause I'm gon' serve the Lord with ease

Can't Keep It To Myself

Some say I am wrong
Because I choose not to stay
In this mental and spiritual prison
That has taken control of my life
Not allowing me to grow
To blossom
Or to move forward into the life
That God has for me.

They keep pulling at me not to change
Because they have become afraid
Afraid of the unknown
because they lack the need
the want
The vision
And the potential to
Want to Move
To seek
To change
To have an intimate relationship with Him

They fail to realize that all power
Lies within Him
He is the giver of life
The Alpha
The Omega
My Strength
My Hope
My Peace
My Joy

They fail to see that
When all else fails
Without any doubt in my heart
He will provide
In my darkest hours I put my trust
In the God that I serve

Nobody can take my love
My joy
Or my relationship
With my savior from me
They can take anything else
But I refuse
To give up

To let go
Of the Trinity
That consists of
The Father
The Son
The Holy Spirit
Because it is the Trinity
That has fulfilled
Me completely.

All of my days consist of
Praise
Worship
Glorification
Edification
and honoring
The Most High God
Because He is worthy
and can't nobody do me like Him.

Can't Be Touched

While most men are walking with their eyes wide shut
I am grinding like I can't be touched
Some say I'm cocky
But I say it's my confidence talking
Swag like mines can't be defined
Replenishing the earth with the fruits
To feed the hungers of those who starve for knowledge
But lack the proper opportunity to seize the moment
To rightfully step into the game and up to the throne
But choose to sit back to watch me navigate this place called earth
As I struggle to alleviate the pressures
Placed upon my shoulders by the world
While methodically plotting my next move
In order to cruise the next events set before me
Carrying the purpose to devastate the lives attached to mines
Leaving me to wonder why cats are more like the librarians
That are used to look me up and research my purpose
But come up with nothing because my story has yet to be told
Due to the mere fact I ain't looking to be sold
I am a treasure that is not to be composed or confined
Within the boundaries of mankind
But to be free to leave my own legacy
A stamp of individuality
Not a replica of what's fresh on the streets today
There is no room for defeat
When it comes to the purpose for which I came to serve
Therefore I strap the weight of my world to my shoulders
Only to grind like I can't be touched

"Now they say sinning is for sinners so I guess I'm not a sinner. Beginnings is for beginners so I guess I'm no beginner"

The Pain Within

Tonight is your night to shine
Let no man put you in a bind
Support or no support
Don't become corrupt
When all else fails
God will be there to prevail
Don't cry-dry your eyes
Those sad tears aren't worth shedding
The things you do is
What brings out the best in you.
Let no man damper your party
your night maybe dreary
But don't let your heart grow weary
your pain is my pain but
we must wait for our time to reign
because our living must not be in vain

This Thing Called Love

Collaboration between Makeisha A. Williams & Brotha Nature

(Makeisha)

2 years 3 months 5 days
Before I be next to you in ecstasy
Can't you see nothing compares to loving me
You plus me equals an eternity
Of loving each other passionately
Devouring the very core of what intimacy should be
Living this thing called love with no expectations
Just a whole lot of reciprocation

(Brotha Nature)

to reciprocate is twice my blessing when I'd expect nothing less,
than the reward of giving out of love which is how blessings manifest,
yes I can see there's no comparison, as well as the potency of the equation,
hearts eagerly parallel for invasion in breeding unbreakable foundation,
the countdown is far from discouragement, more like encouragement,
when duration is not even seconds compared to an eternal nourishment,
on a spree of spontaneous spoiling, specially splendid not speculation
sorrows soothed into sensual stimulation, synonymous to solidification
casting a storm of serenity to wash away any pain,
the question is: "can you stand the rain"?

(Makeisha)

I can embrace the rain
As long as you promise not to change
There won't ever be a need to compare me to the rest
Cause I'll always give you better than my best
Keeping you within my grasp
While knowing that building on what we have will be a task
Refusing to compromise our integrity
Knowing what we have is a rarity
So there is no need to give the world clarity
They lack the knowledge to build
On something that is so real

(Brotha Nature)

That's because realistic love for them appears too far to grasp,
they'd rather follow falsified fantasy scripts than attempt to birth what we have,
indeed a task, yet I'm more focused on long term benefits and a retirement plan,

most importantly, the man above who referenced me and trusted it in my hands,
I can't disappoint HIM, YOU or US nor can see it happening when we're all on the same page,
so with the exception of progression & spontaneous affection you need not worry about change,
even in the last stages, nothing changes, only strengthens and upgrades our caliber,
I'm right there where "I love to be", where I "need to be", as if I'm your catheter,
and STILL exempt from being "pissed off", only embracing what's flowing from you,
when 20 years, 30 months and 50 days prior, it was what I was chosen to do,

(Makeisha)

Which causes your obedience to be greater than your sacrifice
because we both know that everything comes with a price
especially when two hearts are to unite
in order to ignite a future that is beyond bright
due to the refusal of being bound to the norms of a society
that would keep them from being able to the live perpetually free
forcing their alter egos to lie remotely dormant
causing them to explore an abundance of possibilities
of being exclusively intertwined within one mind, one soul, one body
totally causing an explosive combination of forces to perpetuate
a love so strong that others dare not demonstrate

(Brotha Nature)

to demonstrate such an intoxicating substance requires "proof" not an imitation,
most succumb to "quitting", "depression", and even "rehabilitation",
this is GROWN FOLKS love, straight with no chaser, a bit too REAL,
my heart's strong as STEEL, but STILL it was blinded by the STEAL,
intriguing invitation to restoration & remedy resulting from your robbery,
solemnly conditioned to diminish the non-assurance of a "probably"
bright is an understatement, we ignite an incomparable "glow"
with both prepared to be the "G" in front, when either is feeling "low"
conversations converting complications caused by our comforting combination,
complimented by the conglomerate of our chemistry's culmination,
we take minor breaks but immune from fathoming a "break up"
"making up" for those whose hearts masqueraded in players "make up"
our intense intertwining is infallible where impostors were inadequate,
reflecting radiance envious to an immensely-epic establishment

(Makeisha)

Purposely sending all nations into the ultimate shock
knowing that our foundation was planted on a solid "ROCK"
that can't and won't be destroyed
cause this thing we call love could never be null and void
teaching others the importance of a humbling embrace
that is not always about running a human rat race

to see who can be first to catch the bait
but who can truly await to receive what they anticipate
while showing the world what you need lies deeply inside me
cause depth can extend more than what the human eye can see

(Brotha Nature)

That's because its meant to be "felt" just when the eyes may deceive,
just as seeing with the heart convinces what the eyes once didn't believe,
this thing called love I once feared but now can't help but embrace as if compelling,
similar to firearms, it appears dangerous until the NEED for it became overwhelming,
that comes with maturity, yearn to learn, then INCORPORATION
not just being "attracted for what it could do for you", "lack of confidence" and all that dumb shit,
ironically the two are meant to "protect", "defend", "equip" and "advance",
fear comes from the thought of what if it ends up in "the wrong hands",
its not the element but the person who lacks respect for it who contributes these statistics,
when DENIAL or BLAME are at hand to face, its hard when that's too REALISTIC,
when "used against you" vs. "for you", this often leads to apprehension,
the thought of risking placement in such position brainwashes "purpose" beyond "prediction"
what was missing was responsibility, understanding, and CAUTION to inflictions capable,
with you all these elements were presented upfront resulting in a proposal inescapable,
you reflect parallelism in protection, serenity in SAFETY, the foundation most fantasize to muster,
together our knowledge of the hurtful aspects only makes us that much more careful to not rupture

Love Charges

Today I am facing charges
charges that can't and won't be
erased,
defined
or understood
for you see
nobody expected it to be this way
for a person who shows no feelings,
lacks emotions
and possesses a dynamite temper.
Shutting down love each time it swung my way,
due to the demons that tortured my soul
causing me to feel
something time couldn't heal
but with his soft spoken words,
unique but sincere attentiveness
he began to stroke my ego
showing me my true worth
leading to my vulnerability
forcing me to do the unthinkable
loving from the depths of my soul
so I must stand before a juror of my peers
pleading guilty to assault with a deadly weapon called love
knowing the sentence would be 20 to life
for thinking with my HEART and NOT my HEAD

Truth Hurts

As I weep away the pain,
a river begins to form around my soul
as I fold away the memories
that has flooded out my mind
leaving me heavily burden,
shackled down in fear that the love I once felt
will go unkept
needing the strength and wisdom
to walk away
while trapped in a well kept box
disguised by secrecy
lacking the freedom to reveal the truth
cause just like one size fits all,
the truth hurts all involved
but just this once
someone needs to dare to care enough for me
to reveal their truth,
to let my heart be free,
to cherish my worth
for my soul desires to be healed and sealed
but can't be done
without losing two souls
all for the price of one
just because the truth hurts

Second Best

I am the glue that holds you together
but you stuck on treating me as if I am second best
thinking I am gon' be here forever,
if you ain't willing to invest
then I can't keep taking shots to an already broken heart
that you promised to mend
but you was too selfish to start
because there was rules you refused to bend
in order for you to conquer the hurt
that took me by force so you stepped out with her
leaving me no choice but to become defiant
to the laws of the land
but I will be damned if I become a client
to an underpaid defense attorney who couldn't understand my brand
in order to secure me a win
even though the prosecution could prove my guilt
so before I seek revenge,
you better see if our relationship can be rebuilt

Confirmation

I know you ain't blind
because you see all the signs
that she not genuine
but it ain't my place
to state the true case
and be coined as a hater
which is something that ain't in my nature,
I'm just a participator
in something that's greater,
more like a source
that takes over the world by force
but that's beside the point
cause she beating more dicks than niggas in the joint
so don't be surprised if you come up with crabs
that she passed along after freaking the Arabs
while jacking off the clears
for something more than it appears,
yeah I know you think I am wrong
for going harder than Connie Chong
when chasing a story
before she hooked up with Maury
who airs out the dirty laundry of tricks
like the bitch you effing with,
but before you try to blast me
for defining her as nasty,
take a deep look
at her little black book
and you'll see who's the crook,
so don't get mad
cause you should be glad
I'm the one who proved that you been had,
while others woulda been reckless when choosing to divulge the information
that was sure to give you your confirmation
on what you thought was a mutual arrangement
only to find out that she had a sexual fever
that could force an atheist into becoming a Jesus believer
while all others look like sexual underachievers
cause she a deep throat breather
that lacks enough conscience
that would force a heart patient to become unresponsive
so I said all this
to let you know you just another notch on her list…

Love Has No Race

I am that bitch your chick wish she could be
cause I got that power to blow your mind
just like Dre did when he dropped the Chronic Album
but the thing is she couldn't be me
on my worst day even if she tried
cause I am nothing to idolized,
imitated,
or duplicated
more or less emancipated
from the state of competition
forcing me to live life in a repetition
of searching for what I know is meant to be mines
because I am a FIRST place trophy
refusing to settle for second place status
so when a nasty beast of a woman like the one that's on your arm
steps outside of the boundaries
in order to knock me off my throne
I beat them in the face with my charm
cause I see no need to cause them any bodily harm
but I don't know how long I can refrain from being held in your arms
while we both know it's wrong for us to embrace
what we refuse to publicly face
all because it will cause our families public disgrace
just because we decided to love outside of our race

I'm a B.A.D. {{Blessed and Delivered}} Woman. Whenever you got somebody trying to test your last nerve, be a B.A.D. Individual-Makeisha A. Williams

A Soldier's Prayer

As I lay me down to sleep
I pray the Lord my soul to keep
if I should die while duty calls
I pray the Lord watches over my family
for once and for all
for I know the Lord my God
will keep me safe
and give me strength when I am weak.
When I grow weary I pray God holds me near
for He always sees my tears
strengthen me oh Father
when you see me running in fear.
Oh Father, you know my heart is sincere when I say,
bless me this day as you do everyday.
Continue to protect me and my troop
and all the other servicemen too
for a soldiers prayer to serve YOU
and country too.
AMEN!

Born to Die

It has come time for my heart to make a confession
in order to deal with this aggression
that is keeping me bound
from making my normal rounds
spreading the word
of a man whose life was so profound
that every knee shall bow and confess that He is Lord
now you see I am moving toward
telling you about the rewards
of living a life of sanctification
after receiving emancipation
from a life of shame
where we can only take the blame
for partaking in our own sinful fame
 until the day came
when Jesus made His claim
in order for us to change
while we find fault for all the things
that our misfortunes in life brings
without truly seeking God's face
for His perfect grace living
without regards to the pain
that Jesus had to suffer during His reign
which forces my heart to be sick especially when I see
people protesting for a physical victory,
motioning for that final plea
that not even Jesus can't a chance to achieve
when He hung from the cross on Calvary
where they nailed Him to cross,
and pierced Him through His sides
stripping him of His pride
forcing an INNOCENT man to be EXECUTED
for sins He never committed
all because He was BORN to DIE

Redemption's Call

I recognized the look in his eyes
It was one I seen a thousand times
A look that pierced my soul
Inflicting such a pain that the unseen damage
Continually forced me to be incapable
In the arena where I always seemed to be most confident
No longer carrying myself as "The People's Champ"

Drowning in my own sorrows in more ways than one
Causing myself to be unknown while lacking self control
Slipping down a slippery slope into an alcohol induced state
Practically lifeless
Grasping for a piece of consciousness
Reaching for the portion of hope I left clipped with more than a tight grasp
To the very breastplate that covered and protected my heart
Brutally shaken
Unknowingly beaten to a pulp
All because I let him in to a place
Known to be an inflexible space
Unable to comprehend why we couldn't make amends

Tears began to flow as I grasp for my chest
Body convulsing with sobs
Leaving me to be in a moment of distress
Words began to flow from my tongue
As I began to address my sorrows
To the one who listens best
Pleading Him for things that no longer should go unspoken
Yet questioning why I had to be one of the "chosen"

Without neither warning nor regards for my emotional state God began to speak
He spoke loud and clear saying
You were born into royalty because I am the King
But you refused to let me be the reason you sing
While all others deserted you, I was your constant
Time after time I heard your cries
But you have chosen not to realize that your destiny must go uncompromised
My child you must reflect on things I give you in my teachings,
Continue to speak my truths, obey my commands
While not worrying about the things you must sacrifice
Because my word shows you everything comes with a price
So it's up to YOU to STAND STRONG
It's up to YOU to STAND TALL
It's up to YOU to WALK into YOUR CALL

Hell's Gate

As I began to clutch my chest
I knew this pain was much different than the rest
It would determine whether I'd pass the test
So I knew I had to give it my best
For I am much different from the rest
Falling in and out of consciousness
Calling on God for His righteousness
Forcing my heart to confess
That without Him, I'd be nothing but a mess
Just as pictures of my past began to flash
Leaving me wishing I hadn't lived my life so fast
There came a voice from my past
Whispering in my ear
Telling me my time was near
To have no fear
because the Spirit of the Lord was here
I had endured my race
by running at a steady pace
knowing one day I would see God's face
Making myself dependent upon His saving grace
But little did I know
My light had lost its glow
My words were only a show
Despite how I was raised
I failed to get saved
Satan had used me as bait
Wishing it was a dream while walking through Hell's gate.

Death's Beat

Everybody knew Teesha from around the way
Cause she always had something to say
The laws of the land-she just couldn't obey
She paid with her life that hot summer day
Even when things begin to feel a little tight
She didn't give up without a fight
Just so she could prove she was right
Never was she a heathen
But she believed in gettin' even
So once Mook caught her cheatin'
He gave that ass a beaten
That coulda stopped any man from breathin'
They say talk is cheap
But the cost of a life is steep
Cause Teesha laying six feet deep
What we sow, we must reap
But living life confined to a cell
Is something Mook wouldn't live to tell
They beat him til his head begin swell
Just before his body fell

Getting It In

Looks can be deceiving
no wonder my ego took a beating
and my body is steady grieving
cause any other time crack
woulda been whack
but tasting that smack
was all a part of the act
just before he put me on my back
there was no need to slow grind
or press rewind
because eventually I'd get it rough from behind
just as quick as I got a fake ID
he passed off HIV
 leaving me nothing to achieve
but a bunch of hostility
knowing there was no need to conceive
another human being
cause a child shouldn't have to pay for my sins
cause I caught HIV while getting it in

A Woman's Exit

Today I just wasn't me
so blind to see
my own true beauty
which lies beneath
an exterior of cuts and scraps
scars and contusions
not by my own choosing
but by somebody else's abusing,
continually misusing,
and causing confusion,
not allowing me a chance
to take a stance
on the matter at hand
leaving me no other choice
but to file for divorce
because I refuse to have sexual intercourse
with a dude who refuses to get tested for HIV
after he cheats on me with a chick who has herpes
my mama didn't raise no fool
so let me take you to school
and teach you how to be smart when using that tool
because you seem to not be able to follow the rules
when it comes to being faithful
in a nation full
of incurable diseases
that attacks the human body as it ceases
all its vital organs
to make a person incomplete
in more ways than one
all because he chose to have a few nights of fun
without regards of what it would do to my heart
yet he expects me to stay
to make it work out somehow, someway
at the end of day
there is no way I can stay

Flashbacks

For some reason I keep having flashbacks
to the times you was chasing me like I was the best thing since crack
matter of fact your game was whack
but that didn't stop me from indulging just once
which led me to an addiction,
a strenuous fixation,
that would eventually would become a one sided game participation
for there was no longer an importance placed on reciprocation,
dedication,
and damn sure was not one ounce of appreciation
leaving us to cry out for emancipation
and multiple reparations
but refusing to let go
causing both parts more than just devastation,
 lack of concentration,
and no more sexual experimentation
being that we were both on different pages

never will I forget the night I liked to died
all because I was down for the ride
too blind to see that you was trying to kill me
instead of helping to heal me
yea I said
due to the images you kept embedded
in my brain
made me ashamed
of my 500+ pound body frame
because it was nothing but a thang
for you to scream I need to up my weight game
as if I wasn't already causing my heart enough strain
but now that I look back I must admit
I took that hit
cause I was bound
to be down
for a stupid clown
who only caused me to frown

when I started to see
that we could no longer be
you were quick to compare me
to the beast of your past,
you swore that I wanted to live life to fast
cause I wanted to have the gastric bypass
not understanding that I was crushing my heart

as well as being forced to carry oxygen for respiratory support,
I always loved you
but I love me more
so if I gotta leave this earth prematurely
let it be for attempting to save me
rather than trying to live for you
cause once I am gone
there is no coming back
so kick me off your track
cause I know its plenty chicks
who is ready to be with a controlling, vindictive prick
who knows nothing about compromise,
being wise
or how to hang onto the ultimate prize.

Stained Glass

So I heard your voice today
as I began to pray,
immediately I thought my mind
was on automatic rewind
cause it has been so long
since you been gone,
but God knew the only way to get me to listen
was to send someone I had been missing
the more I tried to ignore your voice
the louder you got, leaving me no choice
but to embrace
what you was about to say
as I lay on my face
and continued to pray

Your approach was no different
because it caused me to relive the most current events
especially when I heard you say
"Big Mama, there has to be some other way
 because the strong woman I know would never stay
confined to a situation that forced her to obey
rules and regulations that required her to live against her moral code
or carry more than her load
causing her to break her back
which would eventually lead her to attack
those who have thrown her off track."

Knowing you was about to hit a spot
that was sure to make me hot,
I attempted to dodge your point
but there was no way you was letting up
even if I tried to front
that the situation was something it wasn't
cause you knew I would constantly mask
the details of my redundant task
if you refused to put me on blast

So without giving me a chance to disguise my plan,
you took me to a place which forced you to navigate the land,
showing me that things were to work according to God's will
and if I would just be still
that He would show me how to stay spiritually aligned
leaving me to stand out from the rest of mankind
due to me becoming spiritually blind
to my God approved destiny

cause I seemed to headed towards receiving a spiritual felony
for losing the natural ability
to discern my peers capabilities
that could either leave me limitless,
or powerless
beyond means
that would force me to come clean
in the sight of the Most High
because I refuse to let my soul die
for being too stupid to realize
selling my soul to devil
just to be on the same level
as those who were manifested
with the equivalence of the poisons of cancer
that would eventually spread to the very core of me
if I would continue to let feed my mind, body and soul
with the very immoral code that they choose to believe
by no fault of their own
 but due to being brainwashed
into conforming to the norms of what the majority thought was best
then I would be selling myself short
and setting my soul up for the ultimate spiritual death

Now that I've had these revelations
I know that some things have to change
because I refuse for constraints
to keep me bound to a stage in life
that I had long outgrown
but refuse to move past
because I was stuck looking at my life through stained glass

Fate

My eyes began to bleed tears
when my heart experienced one of its greatest fears
leaving me unable to grasp the brutal fact
that I can't bring you back
knowing that you were a jewel
who lived by God's golden rules,
teaching us to embrace
whatever we would normally be afraid to face
when we operated outside of God's saving grace,
a woman of great faith
who touched lives at enormous rates
issuing out the true essence of love unscripted
so that we wouldn't miss it
forcing us to exemplify the very core of a foundation
which is passed down each generation
in order to unite us as our own nation
so when God called you home on that October day
we would be able to fast and pray
that God would give us the strength to endure the pain
that came with this downpour of rain
so that your memory would not be in vain
leaving your love forever embedded in my heart
where you held a place from the very start
cause you embraced me for all that I am and for all that I ain't
while teaching me not to let my heart grow faint,
to let God be the ruler of my destiny
so that I wouldn't get caught living out a fantasy,
and that God makes no mistakes
cause His mercy is great,
which prepared me for the day
He would take you away,
what some would call fate
but somehow I know you will be entering heaven's gates

Sunshine's Tribute

Tick tock
let's rewind the clock
back to the days when we ran the block
no common blood ran through our veins
but that didn't mean a thang
missing the days we used to hang
possessors of beauty and brains
destining to make a change
forcing our way in the hearts of many
causing dizzy tricks to envy
because their wicked souls were empty
now I'm trying to refrain
from going insane
cause they took you out with a bang
nothing can remove this pain
knowing my heart is left with an empty space
cause I can no longer see your face
or feel your embrace
wishing you was here to wipe away these tears,
telling me what I needed to hear
especially when dealing with fear
my little sista
from anotha mista
had a future so bright
it made dudes uptight
so I know you put up a fight
but it still don't make it right
so when I go to sleep at night
I pray to the Lord above
that I allow my heart to continue to love
while I keep your memory alive
in this struggle to survive

About the Author

Makeisha "Hood Dutchess" Williams is a North Carolina native residing in Alamance County, North Carolina who has been writing poetry since her early teens. She was inspired to put together a collective display of her works based on her life experiences and the experiences of those around her in hopes of reaching as many people as possible. During her free time she is an avid reader and lover of music, who also enjoys promoting and empowering plus sized beauties.

To find out about more about the author of this book please email all inquiries to:

williams.makeisha@ymail.com

To find out more about the artist of the book cover of this book please email all inquiries to:

brotha.nature@gmail.com

www.ingramcontent.com/pod-product-compliance
Lightning Source LLC
Chambersburg PA
CBHW041538220426
43663CB00002B/72